ANIMALS IN DANGER

text by John Malam
designed by Hilary Edwards
colour illustrations by Graham Austin
black and white illustrations by Ray Burrows

Published in Great Britain by World International Publishing Ltd.,
an Egmont Company, Egmont House, PO Box 111,
Great Ducie Street, Manchester M60 3BL.
Printed in Italy.
ISBN 0-7498-0124-7

Are animals in danger?

Can you imagine the world where the only living animal is man? Try and think about it for a while.

There would be no birds in the sky, fish in the sea, or mammals on the land. How different the world would be. You would have no pets at home, zoos and wildlife parks would be empty, there would be no sports such as horse racing, some medicines would have to be made in new ways, we would no longer wear clothes or cosmetics made with help from animals and, of course, we would not eat meat.

It's hard to think of the world without animals. Do you think the world will ever be like this? The answer is that one day it could be – *because animals everywhere are in danger.*

No one knows how many different kinds of animals there are. Scientists can only guess at the real number. There could be as many as 30 million different animals in the world, of which less than two million have been identified. And out of all these kinds of animals as many as 1,000 different kinds could be dying out each year – *which is about three every day.*

But what is putting animals in danger? There are two main causes: loss of habitat and man's ignorance. When a forest is cut down, a field ploughed, a valley flooded or a river polluted, the natural home of the animals that live there is destroyed. And when an animal is over-used by man for his own needs, it may be man's greed that causes that kind of animal to die out.

Animals are in danger, and the danger comes from man – *over 500 different kinds of animals have died out because of man.*

Dodo
A flightless bird from Mauritius, first discovered about 1507. Killed by European settlers and their dogs. Extinct by 1681.

Which animals are in danger?

Scientists divide the animal kingdom into a number of groups, such as mammals, birds, fish, amphibians, reptiles and animals without backbones. In each group there are animals in danger of dying out. But for some it is already too late.

When there are no more animals left alive of a particular kind, scientists say that those animals are 'extinct'.

Great auk
A flightless seabird of the North Atlantic. Killed by hunters for food and bait. Extinct by 1844.

Passenger pigeon
Millions inhabited eastern North America in the early 1800s. Killed by settlers for food. The last passenger pigeon died on September 1, 1914 in the Cincinnati Zoo.

Animals such as the dodo, great auk and the passenger pigeon have all become extinct within the last 300 years, and all because man hunted them or destroyed their habitats.

Today there are about 4,500 animals all over the world facing extinction and scientists are working hard to save them. Time has run out for the animals shown on these two pages – *they are extinct.* But for all the other animals in this book there is still time to save them from dying out for ever.

Mammals in danger

There are more than 4,000 different kinds of mammals, ranging in size from the largest animal that has ever lived, the 150-tonne blue whale, to shrews that weigh only a few grams. Over 550 different kinds of mammals are in danger.

What is a mammal?

It is an animal with a backbone; its young are fed with milk from their mothers; it has hair (even whales in their unborn stage); it is warm-blooded.

Indian tiger

In 1900 there were about 40,000 tigers living in India. By 1969 there were 2,500 and in 1972 only about 1,800. They were being hunted for their skins and at the same time their jungle habitat was being destroyed. The Government of India launched Project Tiger in 1972. Since then the tiger population has risen to about 3,000.

Black rhinoceros

In 1970 there were about 65,000 black rhinos living in Africa. Today there are less than 3,000.

All along the Zambezi valley, in Zimbabwe, wildlife rangers are working to save the black rhino from poachers. The poachers want the black rhino's horn which can be made into dagger handles and even into a medicine by chemists in China.

Blue whale

At the start of this century over 200,000 blue whales were swimming in the world's oceans. Today only about 1,200 are thought to be left.

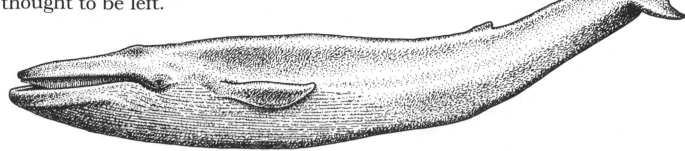

The blue whale has been over-hunted by man, and since 1967 it has been a protected animal. Blue whales live alone or in small groups. When frightened they can swim at up to 37 kilometres per hour.

Giant panda

This is one of the world's best known animals – and one of the rarest. The giant panda lives in the bamboo forests of western China, where there are fewer than 1,000 left alive. Even though the giant panda is protected by law in China, it faces danger from starvation. Sometimes entire bamboo forests die, leaving no food for the giant panda. In 1975 about 150 giant pandas may have died this way.

Mountain gorilla

The jungles and forests of Africa are home to the few mountain gorillas that still survive in the wild. There may be fewer than 300 of these shy animals left. As man clears the forests the mountain gorillas lose their home, and it becomes harder for them to survive. Poachers are also threatening their survival.

More mammals in danger

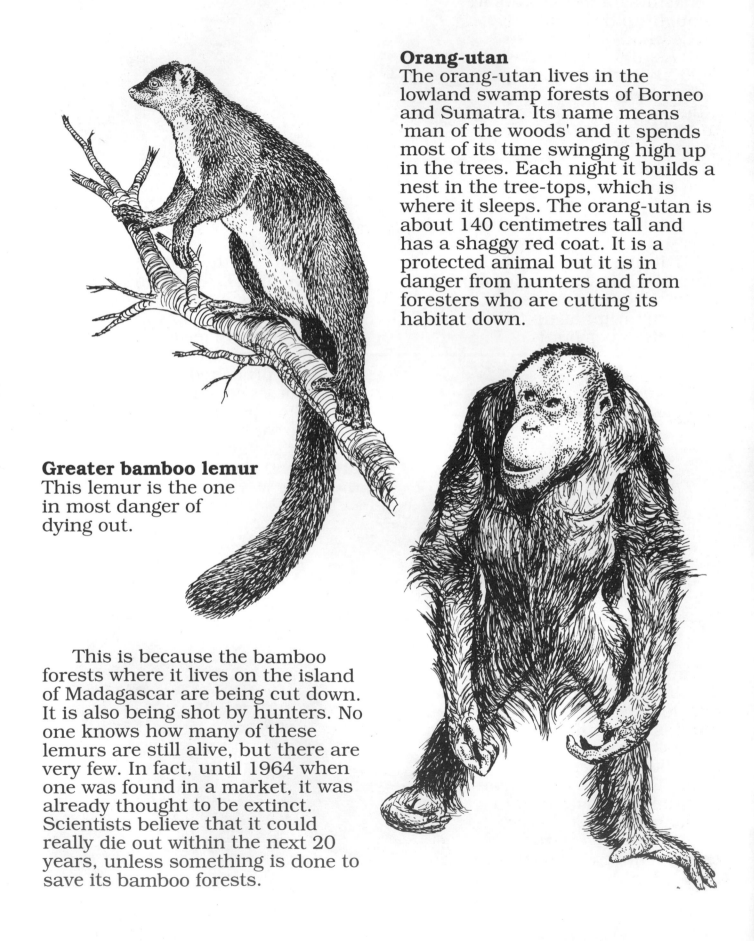

Orang-utan
The orang-utan lives in the lowland swamp forests of Borneo and Sumatra. Its name means 'man of the woods' and it spends most of its time swinging high up in the trees. Each night it builds a nest in the tree-tops, which is where it sleeps. The orang-utan is about 140 centimetres tall and has a shaggy red coat. It is a protected animal but it is in danger from hunters and from foresters who are cutting its habitat down.

Greater bamboo lemur
This lemur is the one in most danger of dying out.

This is because the bamboo forests where it lives on the island of Madagascar are being cut down. It is also being shot by hunters. No one knows how many of these lemurs are still alive, but there are very few. In fact, until 1964 when one was found in a market, it was already thought to be extinct. Scientists believe that it could really die out within the next 20 years, unless something is done to save its bamboo forests.

Indian elephant

This elephant is smaller than the African elephant. The main difference is that its ears are a lot smaller. Its home is amongst the thick jungles and open grasslands of India and south east Asia. It can weigh up to 5,000 kilograms and can eat 200 kilograms of grass a day. In India and Asia these elephants are used at special ceremonies and in the forestry trade. They face danger because their natural habitat is slowly being destroyed.

Giant armadillo

The giant armadillo lives in the tropical parts of South America. It likes open spaces but will also live in forests, feeding on termites, other insects and plants at night. With its strong, short legs and curved claws it digs burrows. It can grow to about one and a half metres long. This strange-looking animal is covered in many plates of armour which protect it from attackers. The giant armadillo is in danger because its habitat is being destroyed.

Snow leopard

The high, snowy mountains of central Asia and India are home to the snow leopard. This big cat can be up to two metres in length and has a coat of long, soft fur which is covered in large dark spots. Until quite recently they had not been photographed in the wild. Snow leopards hunt at night, looking for sheep and cattle. They are very rare animals and only a few still live in the mountains.

Birds in danger

There are more than 9,000 different kinds of birds in the world, ranging in size from a tiny hummingbird weighing less than two grams to the ostrich that weighs up to 150 kilograms. Over 1,000 different kinds of birds are in danger.

What is a bird?
It is an animal with a backbone; it is warm-blooded; it has feathers and wings.

Siberian white crane
Less than 2,000 of these large white birds survive.

In the summer they live and breed in cold and icy Siberia. In the winter they fly south to China and Pakistan. They fly thousands of miles to the wetlands of these two countries and along the way are in constant danger from hunters. When they reach the wetlands they face more danger because farmers are draining the land and destroying the cranes' homes.

Dalmatian pelican
Pelicans were once a common sight on the rivers and lakes of eastern Europe.

Because fish is the favourite food of pelicans, they have been killed by fishermen who think the birds are taking too much. Now only 2,600 of these birds are left. They are also losing their homes because the wet places where they like to live are being drained.

Large blue butterfly

Hermann's tortoise

Blue bird of paradise

Blue whale

Bluefin tuna

European smooth snake

Jackass penguin

Giant panda

Indian elephant

Snow leopard

Mountain gorilla

Natterjack toad

California condor

Roman snail

Medicinal leech

Komodo dragon

Japanese giant salamander

Siberian white crane

Giant clam

Mugger crocodile

California condor

The California condor is nearly extinct. In 1987 there were only 27 still alive, all kept in zoos. They no longer fly in the wild. In the 1940s there may have been 100 alive. Then they lived in the mountains of western North America and fed off the bodies of dead animals. Many of the animals had been shot by hunters, and the condors ate their flesh and the hunters' lead bullets as well. Condors may have died out in the wild from lead poisoning.

Jackass penguin

In the 1930s there were two million jackass penguins living on the islands off the coast of South Africa. Today there are about 170,000 – and they are slowly dying out. Oil is polluting the sea, killing the penguins and their food. Their eggs have been taken for food, and even the soil in which they make their burrows has been taken and used for fertiliser.

Blue bird of paradise

There are very few of these beautiful birds left alive in the forests of New Guinea – a country north of Australia. They have bright blue feathers and two long tail feathers which are prized by hunters. The tribal people of New Guinea wear the feathers in their head-dresses. People in Europe used to wear their feathers, too. There are many other kinds of bird of paradise in New Guinea also in danger from feather-hunters.

Fish and amphibians in danger

There are nearly 20,000 kinds of fish and more than 2,000 kinds of amphibians in the world. The largest fish are sharks, and the great white shark can be up to seven metres long. The largest amphibian is the Chinese giant salamander which weighs up to 65 kilograms. Over 600 different kinds of fish and amphibians are in danger.

What are fish and amphibians?

Fish have backbones; they are cold-blooded; they live in water. Amphibians have backbones; they are cold-blooded; they breathe air; they live on both land and in water.

Coelacanth

In 1938 a large, strange-looking fish was discovered off the Comoro Islands, to the east of Africa. The fish was a coelacanth which scientists thought had died out 70 million years ago. More than 130 of these 'living fossils' have now been caught and killed. No one knows how many coelacanths are still alive. One day they may really die out because they will have all been caught.

Japanese giant salamander

This amphibian is a relative of the giant salamander from China.

It grows up to one metre long and lives in the rushing mountain streams of Honshu, the main island of Japan. It is in danger of dying out because it is killed and used in Japanese medicines. Also, it is losing its natural home because the rivers in which it lives are being blocked by dams.

Devil's Hole pupfish

The name of this strange little fish is longer than the animal itself. Only about 400 of these fish are thought to be alive, all living in one pool at Devil's Hole, in California, North America. The fish eat tiny plants which live in the water, and they die if the plants do not grow. In 1967 the Devil's Hole pupfish nearly died out when its pool started to be drained. It is now a protected animal, but there are so few of them left it is still in danger.

Natterjack toad

This toad is the rarest amphibian in Britain. In 1983 there were about 20,000 of them in the country. It has a smooth skin and runs rather than hops. It likes to live in sandy areas and most live in sand dunes along the north west coast of England. The natterjack toad is a protected animal in Britain, but it still faces danger. Because its home is easily destroyed it could die out if not looked after.

Bluefin tuna

The Atlantic Ocean is home to the bluefin tuna, a big fish eaten in large amounts in Japan. The Japanese believe that the meat from the bluefin tuna is special. They think it will make them rich and live a long life. As more and more of these fish are being caught, the bluefin tuna is slowly dying out. There are less big bluefin tunas in the sea and fishermen are now having to catch smaller tunas.

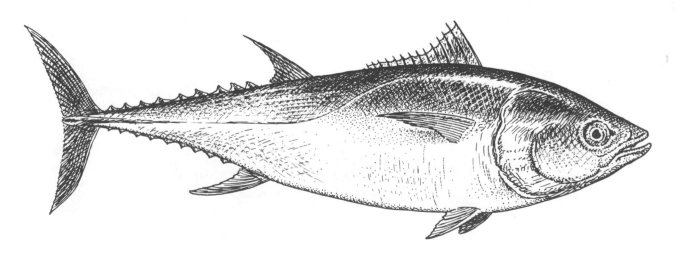

Reptiles in danger

There are about 6,000 different kinds of reptiles living in the world. Snakes, lizards, turtles and crocodiles are all reptiles. Many reptiles, like the dinosaurs, have died out and nearly 200 different reptiles are in danger today.

What is a reptile?

It is an animal with a backbone; it is covered in protective scales; it is cold-blooded; it breathes air.

Komodo dragon

This is the largest lizard in the world and it is found only on three small islands of Indonesia. It can grow to almost three metres long and weighs up to 135 kilograms. The Komodo dragon can live for nearly 100 years. It lives mostly in forests and along beaches, where its burrow is as deep as nine metres. This giant lizard is very rare and it is in danger from hunters.

Hermann's tortoise

This was once a common tortoise in the warm countries of the north Mediterranean, where it lived in sandy burrows. Now it is in danger of dying out in the wild because so many have been collected and sold all over the world as pets. In 1967 more than 450,000 Hermann's tortoises were sold as pets in Britain. Since 1983 they have been protected by a special law and you will not see many in pet shops any more.

European smooth snake

There are three different kinds of snake found in Britain. The smooth snake is the one in most danger. It is a harmless snake whose bite is not poisonous. Unfortunately, many people do not know this and they kill it thinking it can hurt them. The smooth snake lives mostly in the south of Britain and grows up to 75 centimetres long. It likes to lie in sunny places or under piles of stones and it eats small lizards and mice.

Tuatara

This lizard is related to the tuataras which lived 200 million years ago. Now there are only a few of them left alive in some remote parts of New Zealand. It grows up to 70 centimetres long and lives in a burrow. In New Zealand it was once hunted by the Maoris for food, but now it is a protected animal. The tuatara is active at night and it eats insects, small animals and birds' eggs.

Mugger crocodile

There are about 12 different kinds of crocodile in the world, and the mugger crocodile is the one in most danger. It lives in the swamps, lakes and rivers of India, Sri Lanka and Burma. It also likes to bask on land in the sun. Once it was a sacred animal and it was kept in temples and looked after by priests. It is in danger of dying out because it is killed for sport and money. Its skin is valuable and is sold to make clothes, bags and belts.

Other kinds of animals in danger

The largest group in the animal kingdom is made up of animals which have no backbones. These are called invertebrate animals and there are millions of different kinds. The animals in this group include starfish, spiders, crabs, worms, butterflies, snails, sponges and octopuses. No one knows how many animals belong in this group, and there are millions yet to be discovered. Some will have died out before they have even been found.

Medicinal leech

Leeches are a kind of worm which live in water. There are about 300 different kinds and some can grow up to 20 centimetres long. The medicinal leech was once common in Europe where it lived in fresh water and fed on other animals' blood. It got its name because it was once used by doctors to suck blood from their patients. People with headaches would let leeches suck their heads, hoping their headaches would go. Since doctors stopped using leeches the medicinal leech has become rare, and is now in danger of dying out.

Giant clam

The giant clam is an animal in danger of dying out because people want its shell. In some parts of the world the clam's meat is also eaten. The shell can grow to as much as one metre across. Giant clams are found mostly in the Pacific Ocean and even though it is a protected animal it is still being taken from the sea.

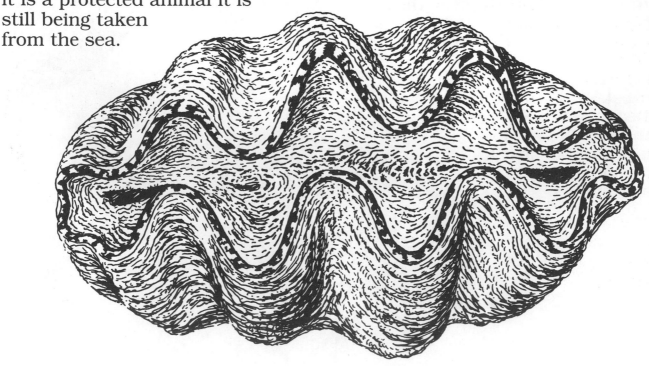

Roman snail

There are more than 100 different kinds of snails found in Europe. One which is in danger of dying out in the wild is the Roman snail.

This is the largest snail found in Europe and its light brown shell can grow to five centimetres long. It lives in woods and hedges. Because this snail is eaten by man, it has already died out in Poland, Holland and Switzerland. In France there are snail farms where it is bred for food.

Large blue butterfly

In 1979 this beautiful butterfly died out in Britain, but it can still be found in other parts of Europe. Once it had been a common sight on the grassy meadows and pastures in the south of Britain where its caterpillars fed on wild thyme and ants. The large blue butterfly has wings of about 35 millimetres across. It died out in Britain because the meadows and pastures were being dug up, which destroyed its habitat. Also, butterfly collectors killed many. In 1983 and 1988 attempts were made to bring this butterfly back to Britain.

Horseshoe crab

This primitive animal is related to scorpions and extinct animals called trilobites. It is a 'living fossil' and lives in shallow water off the coasts of Asia and North America. The horseshoe crab grows up to 50 centimetres long and lays eggs in holes it digs on beaches. It is in danger of dying out because people collect it for food when it comes ashore to lay its eggs. In some parts of the world it is killed and used as fertiliser.

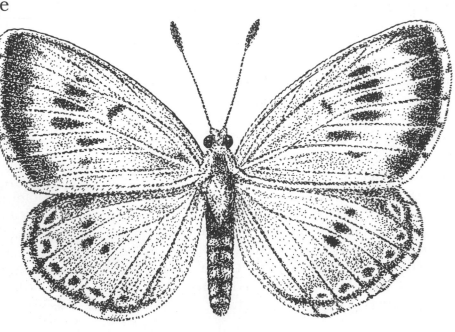

A dangerous animal

There is one last animal to talk about. This animal is not in danger of dying out – *there are over five billion living in the world.* That's over 5,000,000,000,000!

But when we think about all the different kinds of animals in the world which really are in danger of dying out, we must also think about this other kind of animal. It is the one which is putting other animals in danger, yet it is also the one which can save animals from extinction.

Do you know this animal? There's one reading this book now, and there's one hiding in the drawing – *colour the dotted shapes to find it.*

How you can save animals

Saving animals from danger is important – and you can help.

Remember that animals are dying out because of man. The homes of animals all over the world, their natural habitats, are being destroyed. Fields are being ploughed up, forests are being cut down, and rivers and lakes are being polluted.

The fields, trees and rivers near where you live are home to all sorts of animals, even though you may never have seen the animals which actually live there. If you find out that these places are going to be destroyed, then you might be able to save animals by helping to rescue them.

The three organisations listed here are all involved in saving animals. If you would like to know more about how you can help, write and ask for details.

Jersey Wildlife Preservation Trust
Les Augrès Manor
Trinity
Jersey
Channel Islands

World Wide Fund for Nature UK
Panda House
11–13 Ockford Road
Godalming GU7 1QU

Young People's Trust for the Environment and Nature Conservation
95 Woodbridge Road
Guildford GU1 4PY